No Nonsense
Phonics

Boats and Ships

Elizabeth Nonweiler

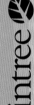
raintree

sailing ship

yawl

airboat

float tube

launch

steamer

hovercraft

lifeboats

dugout boat

fishing trawler

lighters

oil tanker

Interesting facts about the pictures

page 2: **Sailing ships** have masts to hold up sails. Wind blows on the sails to move the ship forwards. This is the *Star of India*. It is the oldest sailing ship still sailing regularly now.

page 3: **Yawls** are boats with two masts for sails – one big and one smaller. They are used mainly for fun or racing. In 1959 John Guzzwell sailed around the world in a yawl called *Trekka*.

page 4: **Airboats** are good for shallow or marshy water, because they have flat bottoms that will not get stuck easily. They have propellers like on aeroplanes at the back to move them forwards.

page 5: **Float tubes** are small boats that you inflate (blow up). People use them for fishing, because they can reach more fish than from land. They sit on a seat, but their legs are in the water.

page 6: A **launch** is a large motorboat that carries passengers a short way on a lake or river. This launch is taking people for a trip on the River Thames in London.

page 7: This **steamer** is called the *Waverley* and is from Scotland. It has a steam engine that drives paddle wheels. It is the only paddle steamer in the world that still goes out to sea now.

page 8: A **hovercraft** can travel over land, water, mud or ice, because it moves on a cushion of air that it blows out from underneath. This one takes people to and from the Isle of Wight.

page 9: **Lifeboats** are small boats kept on big ships for emergencies. If this ship begins to sink, the yellow lifeboats will be lowered into the water and the passengers will get into them.

page 10: **Dugout boats** are made from logs. The bark is taken off, the wood in the middle is burnt and taken out and then the inside is smoothed with a knife. There were dugouts 8,000 years ago.

page 11: **Fishing trawlers** are boats that pull huge fishing nets through the water to catch fish for supermarkets to sell. They have freezers to keep the fish cold and fresh.

page 12: **Lighters** are for taking things or passengers from ocean-going ships to landing places big ships cannot reach. These cranes are unloading containers from lighters in Hong Kong.

page 13: **Oil tankers** carry oil from places that take oil from the ground, to places that refine it (make it ready to use). Tankers also take oil to places where it is sold as fuel for cars or electricity, or for making plastic.

Letter-sound correspondences

Level 2 books cover the following letter-sound correspondences.
Letter-sound correspondences highlighted in green can be found in this book.

ant	big	cat	dog	egg	fish	get	hot	it
jet	key	let	man	nut	off	pan	queen	run
sun	tap	up	van	wet	box	yes	zoo	

duck	fish	chips	sing	thin this	keep	look moon	art	corn
say	boy	rain	oil	boat	eat	pie	high	
make	these	like	note	flute tube	blue cue			
her	bird	turn	airport	flew stew	out	saw	author	when